A GIFT FOR:

_____

FROM:

_____

NOT GUILTY BY REASON OF
MENOPAUSE

LEIGH ANNE JASHEWAY-BRYANT

CELESTIAL ARTS
Berkeley | Toronto

You might be menopausal if...

Your
little black dress
is made from
TERRY CLOTH.

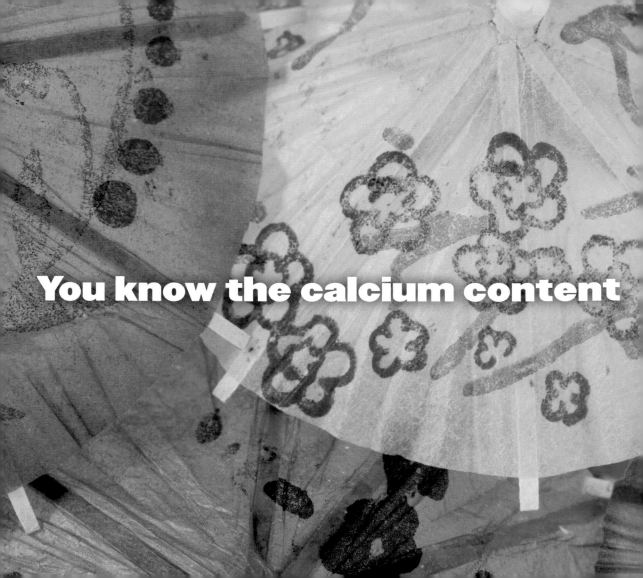

You know the calcium content

in a pitcher of piña coladas.

YOU USE SO MUCH MOISTURIZER THAT YOU SLIDE OFF THE FURNITURE.

you refer to your best friend as

HELLO
my name is

What's Her Name

Ever since the doctor took you off hormones, you've been wearing a nicotine patch, a motion sickness patch, and a bicycle patch.

You add
powdered fiber
to beer.

Your husband dumps ice water on you, and you consider it foreplay.

You keep getting thank-you notes
from the local homeless shelter
for all the blankets you've donated.

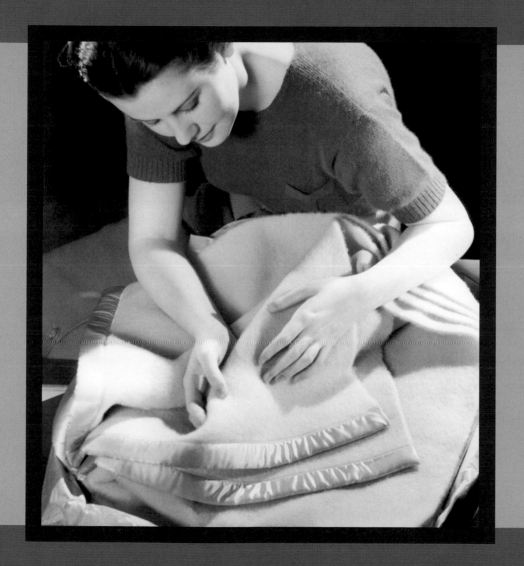

Lo siento
Het spijt me
Es tut mir Leid
Lamento
Mi dispiace
Je suis désolé
ごめんなさい
Jag är ledsen

Your husband has learned how to say

I'm sorry

in eight different languages.

You eat your frozen dinner before it thaws.

You refer to your youngest child as

"MY
LAST FERTILE
EGG."

The pregnancy indicator stick reads,

"YOUR GUESS IS AS GOOD AS MINE!"

You scare your kids
more than they scare you.

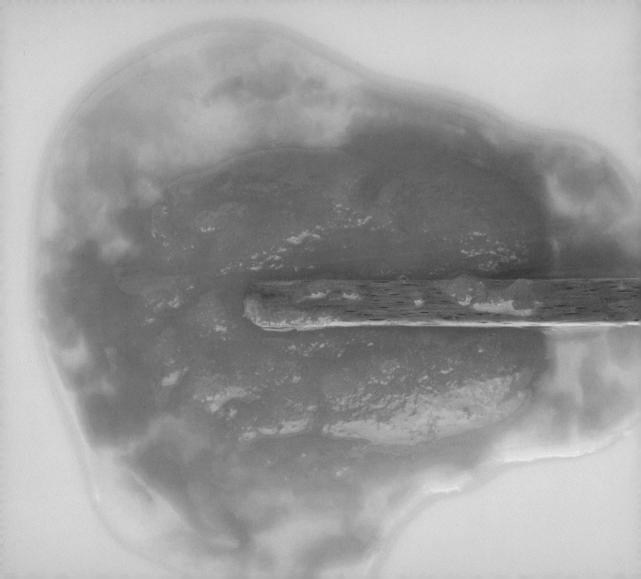

You know
that a Popsicle
can cool you off
in more ways
than one.

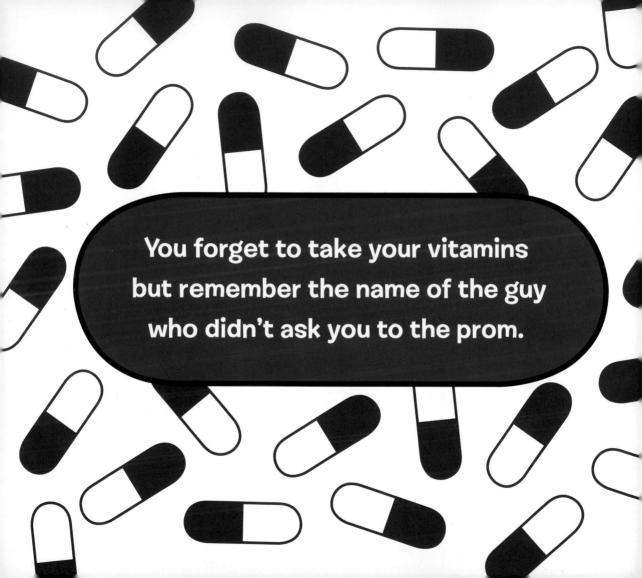

Once a month you fake

PMS.

is the theme from JAWS.

You wear a miniskirt and high heels to buy your mom's bladder

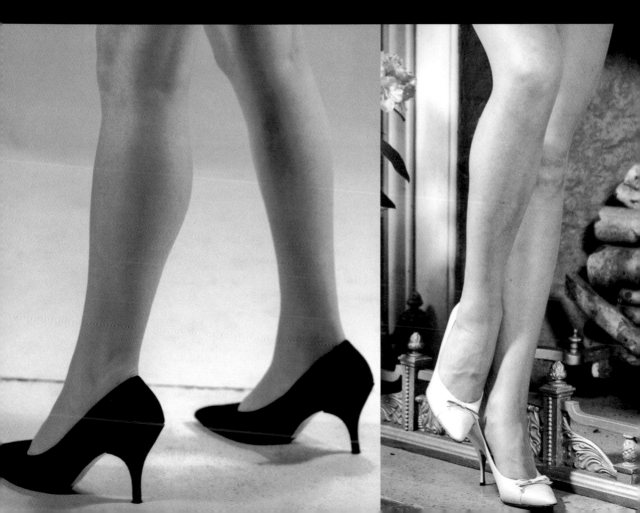

Control underwear so the cashiers don't think they're for you.

Your husband wears a cup to bed.

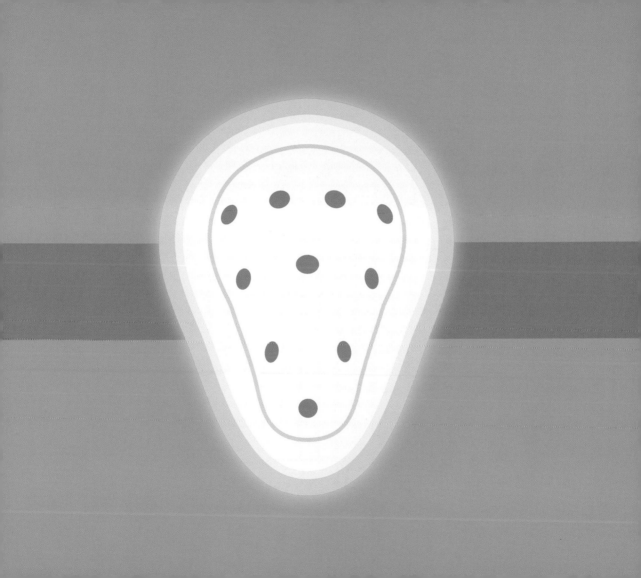

You're not getting back on your scale until gravity shifts back to normal.

You have a recipe for

soybeans and wieners.

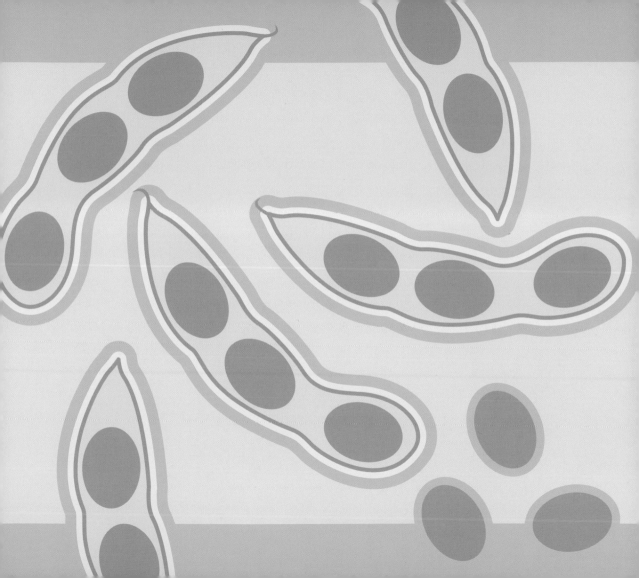

You hire a towel boy.

YOU BUY
RAWHIDE CHEWS,
BUT YOU DON'T OWN A
DOG.

You know you'll never eat for two again—
and that makes you hungry.

You put cayenne pepper
in everything you cook
so your family will stop
turning up the thermostat.

You recently held up a pharmacy
with a note that said,
"GIVE ME ALL YOUR HORMONES
AND NO ONE GETS HURT!"

Despite joining the Witness Protection Program, you've been tracked down by the AARP.

You consider sleeping to be a weight-bearing exercise.

You've done millions of stomach

crunches, but only your floor is flatter.

You binge on milk,
hoping the cows it came from
were injected with hormones.

When you say

"My friend is visiting,"

there are actually suitcases
in your guest room.

Now that there's
no chance of you being pregnant,
people keep asking you
if you are.

YOU'VE DISCOVERED THAT
MELTING PLASTIC DOLLS
IS A GREAT WAY
TO MANAGE STRESS.

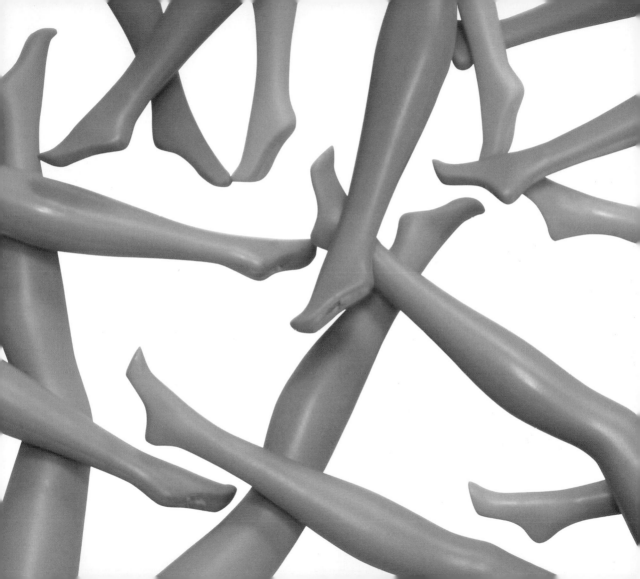

Last Halloween you dressed up as
Lizzy Borden.

SWEAT

YOU

OUT YOUR

.

You tell all your children they're not your favorite.

You Find the 11 g		17%
Labels on 7 g		35%
Chocolate Bars to Be 0 g		
Steamier Than 5 mg		1%
Romance 25 mg		1%
Novels 27 g		9%

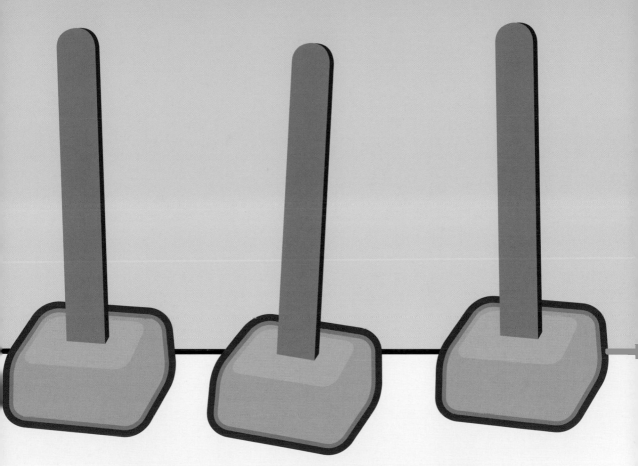

You make candy apples with those caramel calcium chews.

You don't do extreme sports because they pale in comparison to your mood swings.

YOU WEAR *thong underwear . . .*

BECAUSE IT'S COOLER.

LL THE STATION TO CORRECT T

PE RUNNING ACROSS THE SCREE

EEN • WHEN YOU WATCH THE NE

NEWS, YOU CALL THE STATION

TO CORRECT THE GRAMMAR USE

USED IN THE TICKER TAPE RU

HEN YOU WATCH THE NEWS, YOU

TICKER TAPE RUNNING ACROSS WHEN YOU WATCH THE NEWS, YOU CALL THE STATION TO CORRECT THE GRAMMAR USED IN THE TICKER TAPE RUNNING ACROSS THE SCREEN ● WHEN YOU WATCH THE NEWS, ALL THE STATION TO CORRECT

You think about the

'Til death do us part

line in your wedding vows

a little too often.

There's nothing
embarrassing for the
dog to drag out
of the bathroom trash.

You can **hallucinate** without drugs.

YOU BUY SHEETS NOT BY

thread count...

...BUT BY *absorbency*.

You recently stole
a dozen backless
paper gowns to wear
around the house.

The last time you used
a maxi pad with wings was
to make an angel for
the top of the Christmas tree.

You buy antiperspirant in six-packs.

You show up as a hotspot on
satellite weather maps.

*Your book club is
just an excuse to sit around
and drink soy milk.*

6'0"

5'6"

You can pick your

5'0"

4'6"

4'0"

6'0"

5'6"

colon out of a lineup.

5'0"

4'6"

4'0"

You could play Thelma AND Louise in the sequel.

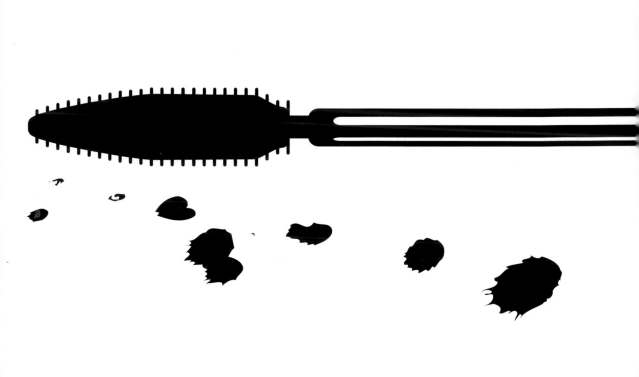

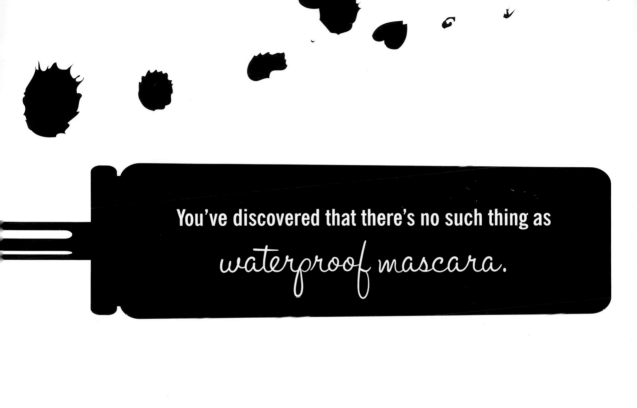

You've discovered that there's no such thing as

waterproof mascara.

You know how much ice cream it takes to get your RDA of calcium.

Photographs on front cover (clockwise from top left) by Getty Images/ Digital Vision; Martin Diebel / Getty Images/fStop; George Marks / Getty Images/Retrofile RF; Rachel de Joode / Getty Images/fStop; Christopher O Driscoll © istockphoto.com; Chris Amara / Getty Images/Digital Vision.

Photograph on back cover by George Marks / Getty Images/Retrofile RF.

Photographs on pages 4, 7, 11, 14–15, 19, 27, 33, 36, 37, 44, 51, 54, 55, 60, 63, 70, 75, 86, 90, 95, and 103 by George Marks / Getty Images/ Retrofile RF.

Photograph on pages 8–9 by Halfdark / Getty Images/fStop.

Illustrations on pages 13, 16, 17, 20, 24, 25, 30, 31, 39, 42–43, 47, 72–73, 76, 77, 82–83, 96, 104–105, and 108–109 by Betsy Stromberg.

Photograph on pages 22–23 by Getty Images/Image Source.

Photograph on pages 28–29 by Getty Images/Westend61.

Photograph on pages 34–35 by Stephen Ramsey / Getty Images/ Uppercut RF.

Photograph on page 40 by Jim Arbogast / Getty Images/Digital Vision.

Photograph on page 47 by Jennifer Borton © istockphoto.com.

Photograph on page 48 by Rachel de Joode / Getty Images/fStop.

Photograph on page 52 by Getty Images/Stockbyte Silver.

Photograph on pages 58–59 by Bill Noll © istockphoto.com.

Photograph on page 65 by Pnc / Getty Images/Photodisc.

Photograph on page 66 by Matthias Tunger / Getty Images.

Photograph on page 69 by Eva Serrabassa © istockphoto.com.

Photographs on pages 78, 99, and 106–107 by Getty Images/Stockbyte.

Photograph on pages 80–81 by Christopher O Driscoll © istockphoto.com.

Photograph on pages 84–85 by Mike Bentley © istockphoto.com.

Photograph on page 89 by Chris Amaral / Getty Images/Digital Vision.

Photograph on pages 92–93 by Oktay Ortakcioglu © istockphoto.com.

Photograph on page 100 by Stocktrek Images / Getty Images/Collection Mix: Subjects.

Photograph on page 106 by Getty Images/Digital Vision.

Photograph on page 110 by Martin Diebel / Getty Images/fStop.